EXCITING
bali

a visual journey

D1604494

EXCITING
bali
a visual journey

Photography by Ian Lloyd
Text by Patrick R. Booz

PERIPLUS

ISBN 962-593-210-0

Printed in Singapore

Distributors

Asia Pacific: Berkeley Books Pte Ltd,
5 Little Road, #08-01, Singapore 536983

Indonesia: PT Wira Mandala Pustaka,
Jl. Kelapa Gading Kirana, Blok A14 No. 17, Jakarta 14240

Japan: Tuttle Publishing,
RK Bldg, 2nd Floor 2-13-10 Shimo-Meguro,
Meguro-Ku Tokyo 153 0064.

North America, Latin America and Europe:
Charles E. Tuttle Co., Inc.,
RRI Box 231-5, North Clarendon, VT 05759-9700

Publisher: Eric M. Oey
Photographer: Ian Lloyd
Writer: Patrick R. Booz
Editor: Nick Wallwork
Designers: Joan Law Design & Photography

Front cover photographs, clockwise from top left:
The *kebyar duduk* dance, first performed in the 1930s and made
internationally famous by the dancer I Mario, a native of Tabanan;
a *barong* dancer at Batubulan; verdant rice terraces against the
backdrop of Mt Agung.

Back cover photographs, clockwise from top right:
Bali is a major surfing destination; the *kecak* dance, also known as
the monkey dance; a fine example of temple architecture; part of an
offering called a *tjili*, made of moulded, fried and dyed rice flour.

Title spread
*A lone temple was built on the
shore of Lake Bratan to venerate
the Goddess of the Waters.
Rituals and celebrations take
place here for the blessing of
irrigation water, which flows
from this high-altitude lake to
nourish rice fields far below.*

Right
*Dawn comes up behind Lake
Batur. This lake lies inside one
of the world's largest volcanic
basins, surrounded by a
mountain rim that measures 13
kilometres (eight miles) across.
In the centre is Gunung Batur, a
holy volcano, second only in
importance to Gunung Agung,
mother-mountain of Bali.
Batur's awesome power has
been felt twice this century, and
these eruptions finally forced
the inhabitants to leave their
villages by the lake and resettle
high above on the mountain
rim, safe from the gas, ashes and
molten lava.*

Pages 6-7
*The temple of Tanah Lot stands
out against a salmon-coloured
sunset on the southwest coast
of Bali. Situated on an isolated
promontory, this is one of the
island's important sea temples
where the spirits and dwellers of
the deep are honoured.*

Pages 8-9
*Hard work and year-round care
are necessary to maintain these
beautiful terraced rice fields. In
the countryside, life's activities
centre around rice, and villages,
hidden away in groves of trees,
are invariably close to the fields.*

Pages 10-11
*Children play in the golden
light of Kuta Beach. Free and
self-reliant at an early age,
children are raised by a liberal
hand at home and learn from
nature in their games and in
their daily forays to seashore,
fields and mountain slopes.*

Page 12-13
*A colourful crowd, united in
common devotion, comes to
celebrate a temple festival. It is
the* odalan, *the birthday of the
temple's founding, and the
whole village attends, dressed in
finest clothing. The festivities,
lasting for a day and a night,
mark a fresh beginning for the
temple year.*

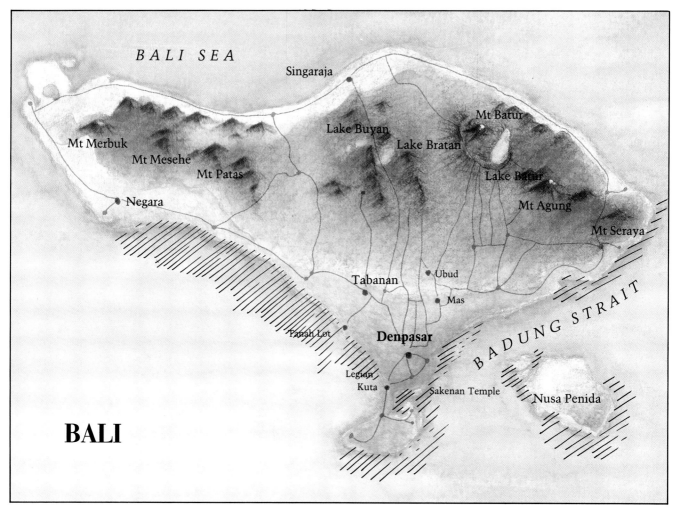

BALI SEA

Singaraja

Lake Buyan

Mt Batur

Lake Bratan

Mt Merbuk

Mt Mesehe

Lake Batur

Mt Patas

Mt Agung

Negara

Mt Seraya

Tabanan

Ubud

Mas

BADUNG STRAIT

Tanah Lot

Denpasar

Legian

Kuta

Sakenan Temple

Nusa Penida

BALI

INTRODUCTION

THE ISLAND OF Bali is just one of thousands of islands in the Malay Archipelago, that great chain that straddles the equator from New Guinea to the tip of Sumatra and once, eons ago, formed a land bridge between Asia and Australia. Yet unlike the other islands, Bali has held sway in the world's imagination for most of this century. Bali's special reputation came about for several reasons, but to the visitor its allure and fascination are clear and immediate. The island is physically beautiful and the people, lithe, graceful and full of friendliness, exude a quiet confidence.

To the Balinese, their island is the entire world. Other worlds may exist outside, but theirs is complete and whole in itself, a total provider, bountiful with all the physical and spiritual attributes important to existence. In fact the Balinese cosmos is so rich that the psychic, unseen world is constantly spilling over into the mundane. Daily life is a constant, vibrant expression of the need to honour, praise and propitiate gods and nymphs, demons and witches. Hardly a day goes by without a procession or temple festival, and at night villages far and wide come alive to opera and dance-drama, accompanied by the strange, hypnotic music of *gamelan* percussion orchestras. To an outsider, Balinese life seems to be a continuous celebration with brief intervals for rest.

According to legend, Bali originated as a special event during the creation of the universe. Through the purity of meditation the phenomenal world emerged, magnificently arrayed, layer upon layer, from the base of the cosmos below to the perfumed heavens above. In between, the island of Bali appeared, resting on an immense turtle afloat in a vast ocean.

The scientific explanation of the island's birth and development is a wonderful story as well. Once connected to the massive Asiatic mainland, Bali became an island after the melting of the polar ice caps nearly 120 million years ago. Bali is considered the last outpost of mainland Asia, separated by a 305-metre deep (1,000-foot) channel from the island of Lombok to the east. This channel also represents an ecological boundary known as the Wallace Line after the 19th-century naturalist Alfred Russell Wallace. He noted that Bali has luxurious tropical vegetation and animals such as elephants, tigers, monkeys and wild cattle, while Lombok and islands to the east suggest an affiliation with Australia and not Asia. Here, east of the Wallace Line, the climate is more arid and the vegetation thorny and scrub-like. The animals include primitive marsupials, the world's largest lizards, parrots and cockatoos and relatively few insect species.

Bali is just over 5,181 square kilometres (2,000 square miles) in area, barely one-quarter the size of Wales, and densely populated with nearly three million inhabitants. Its tropical richness and the ingenious use of terraced rice fields allow the land to support such overcrowding. Elaborate systems of irrigation bring water from the high volcanoes to the shimmering emerald-green fields found in most corners of the island. Rice is the most important food in Bali; the crop is the source of life and wealth and is recognized as a gift from the gods. Legend tells that rice first appeared on Bali when the male God of Water raped Mother Earth to beget rice. Wet-rice farming has existed on Bali for well over 1,000 years, and today's amazing, contoured landscape is the heritage of 50 generations of farmers.

The need to tend the rice and care for the fields led to the rise of the *desa*, or village, the chief social unit in Bali. It is much more than just a village, however; it is community, parish and focal point of all life for the Balinese. Cozy and safe within a lush grove, surrounded by walls and bountiful trees — coconut, banana, papaya, bread-fruit — the *desa* functions to maintain the cosmic balance and harmony within the area of its jurisdiction, thus assuring the well-being of all. Every *desa*, and

Portraits of Balinese men. In the tropical weather people dress for comfort and ease, though there are flourishes that add colour and style to each person's appearance. Men wear the udeng, a square piece of cloth tied into a turban. Each man ties it in a different way, to create a distinctive, individual style.

there are hundreds of them spread throughout the island, is thus seen to be fulfilling its obligation to gods and men.

Bali has often been called 'Land of the Many Temples'. Temples, from small shrines in the rice fields to magnificent complexes belonging to large towns, are certainly the single most important institution on the island, and they can be seen everywhere. By the sea, on desolate promontories, in caves, on the highest mountains, even entangled in the roots of banyan trees, large and small temples appear as a natural complement to the island's geography.

From earliest times, before the overwhelming influence of Hindu temple building arrived from Java a thousand years ago, there have been special places, plots of consecrated ground, where altars, cairns and stone enclosures marked a kind of primitive temple. Such temples still can be seen in the eastern part of the island where isolated villages protected these old forms.

Every Balinese community has at least three main temples: the foundation temple of the original village, often hundreds of years old, a town temple for communal celebrations, and the temple of the dead for the gods associated with death and cremation. The reason for this division is to maintain a sacred balance between the innumerable, contending forces of the invisible world, which to the Balinese has a trenchant reality.

It is difficult to know exactly how many large temples exist on Bali. An attempt to count them was once made after the devastating earthquake of 1917, when 2,431 temples were completely destroyed in one district. This district was moderately populated and comprised about one-ninth of the island's surface area. From this it was deduced that Bali had at least 20,000 important temples at the time, and today, if anything, the number has grown.

The language of Bali is of the Austronesian family, a vast and diverse group of languages that extends from Hawaii and Easter Island in the east to Taiwan, the islands of Indonesia and Madagascar in the west. Balinese is more closely related to the languages and dialects of its eastern neighbours than to Javanese, the tongue spoken to the west by nearly 80 million people. Nevertheless, Old Javanese and Sanskrit have greatly influenced Bali's vocabulary, much as Latin and French have contributed to English.

The outstanding characteristic of Balinese is the use of 'vocabularies of courtesy', a linguistic phenomenon that developed with the introduction of Hindu caste hierarchies. There are in fact three special vocabularies within the one main language. Common speech is used between friends and intimates and employed when speaking to a person of lower social standing. The polite form is spoken to strangers (before their rank is known) and to superiors. The deferential form is employed when speaking to high caste persons, priests and other important people. Misuse of these three vocabularies, whether through ignorance or arrogance, is a serious *faux pas*, and in certain extreme, but rare, cases could result in a court case and punishment.

In spite of these special vocabularies and the traditional, strict adherence to social rank through caste, daily interaction between people is remarkably frank and easygoing. There is a universal sense of happiness and gentleness among the Balinese, and their polite ways and deference are thoroughly natural and unaffected.

Art and ritual are the living breath of the Balinese. There have been times and places in the West, in Renaissance Florence for example, where people expected beauty in their surroundings, where they talked and gossiped about artists endlessly, and where they appreciated and demanded high artistic standards. Such ways have always been the way of the Balinese; nearly everyone, high or low, man or woman, young or old, is engaged and competent in an art or a craft. Technically speaking the words 'art' and 'artist' do not exist in the Balinese language, which is perhaps a reflection of the universal involvement of Balinese with some form of aesthetic expression. Although a great painter or carver is recognized as such, and given pride of place in the community, he or she is not part of a separate class of artists, but is instead no different from a farmer, clerk or simple labourer.

Hand in hand with this casual and self-effacing attitude towards talent, where the greatest good is simply to create something beautiful for the community, the temple or the gods, is the ephemerality of Balinese art. Tropical decay is constantly at work. Wooden posts and statues are the prey of insects, rain and humidity destroy paper and cloth, the sun and heat assure that lovingly made offerings of palm fronds, fruit and flowers last only a day. Even stone carvings have a relatively short life. Sandstone and lava, soft and friable, are the only materials available and, after a few years, the friezes and intricate sculptures into which they have been shaped become unrecognizable. There is a constant need to recreate, replace and rebuild, which makes for the freshness and everlasting youth of Balinese art.

A carved dancer forms part of a temple relief.

The Balinese look back proudly to a glorious past of rajas, princes and heroines, times that brought them their traditions and laid the foundations for a remarkable, vibrant society. Confident in their origins and world view, they have never suffered from stagnation, and their very openness to influences beyond their world has helped to create a special, eclectic mind and aesthetic. Absorption, adaptation and flux have always been a part of Balinese life, an ongoing source of creativity. Influences from Southeast Asia, India, Java, China, Europe, and now even Australia and America, have touched Bali to greater or lesser degrees, leaving their imprint on the people and the art, but they always are transformed in a uniquely Balinese way, with zest, vigour, colour and, frequently, humour. Where else but in Bali could you have an outrageous painting of anthropomorphic frogs snapping away with their cameras? Or a new wall carving on a 16th-century temple showing fat Dutchmen in an automobile?

Amidst the playfulness is a deeper, darker side to Balinese life. In various forms of expression, but usually in that of the dance-drama, the Balinese express the deepest concerns of their collective unconscious. These have to do with struggles between good and evil, strong and weak, clean and unclean.

The powerful and dreaded Rangda, widow-witch and queen of evil spirits, stands at a temple entrance.

Dance and drama are a united form in Bali and do not occupy separate spheres as in the West. They grew out of a religious tradition and in most cases still have religious importance. Entertainment of the deity with dance and music is as natural to the Balinese as the presentation of offerings.

Dance in Bali also brings delight to the people and fulfills many needs and purposes. The *baris* dance, for example, is full of martial expression and gives vent to manly virtues and preoccupations. The *legong*, probably Bali's finest dance, is highly refined and feminine and appreciated on a purely aesthetic level. The *kebyar* is a solo performance of brilliant showmanship. Fun and flirtation are the soul of the *joged* and *janger*, and a wide range of historical and mythic epics find expression in the *topeng* masked dramas and *wayang* shadow puppet plays.

Dances that involve trance, however, lie at the core of the Balinese. Here contact is made with the unseen, and fragile humans become heroic as they enter into the world beyond. In the dance called *sangyang*, young girls bring luck and protective magic to the temple and village. They are the psychic adventurers who go over to the other side to bring back news of the gods, to convey their wishes and moods. Even death itself is approached. As intermediaries and confidants of the deities, they return and help bind together the community by sharing the experience of their contact. They reassure everyone by showing that awesome, unknown mysteries can be faced and survived.

Painted stone carving of a priest holding his sacred bell.

An animal offering, with scarf around its neck, arrives for the start of a purification ceremony. Mirrors, banners and painted, tooled leather adorn a bull in north Bali. Bull races highlight the festival which is held to prepare the fields before planting new rice.

Every young dancer is rigorously trained under the care of a special teacher, himself more than likely a once-famous performer. But the hidden stresses and unpredictability of trance dancing sometimes erupt into wild and frenzied displays that abandon all discipline and only permit order once exhaustion overtakes the dancers. In times of turmoil, some villages will hold trance dances night after night to keep the land calm. Expression of the deities' will, in whatever form, is seen to be a purgative and a balm.

The uses of trance can serve other ends as well. It might be 'discovered' through a trance intermediary that the god in one village is the mother of a god in another. A procession of visitation must take place, and, intentionally or not, two places are brought closer together, old feuds set aside. Trance can also legitimate political movements by revealing the 'correctness' of a particular ideology, and it sometimes explains new developments or strange occurrences, such as natural calamities, that confound a community.

The most powerful use of trance, and the most magically dangerous dance-drama, takes the form of a titanic struggle between the forces of good and evil. Nothing short of humanity's welfare is at stake.

This is the symbolic play of Barong and Rangda, Bali's two most remarkable creatures. The Barong is a benevolent, mystical beast, Lord of the Forest, who intercedes on behalf of mankind to fight disease, black magic and all forms of pollution. His adversary is the hideous Rangda, witch-widow, child-eater and Queen of Death. Barong enters first, dancing and prancing, played by two men hidden beneath a holy mask and lion's body. Rangda then appears with a terrifying fanged mask, its flaming tongue hanging far down between two grotesque pendulous breasts. Fighting begins and the course of battle shifts from side to side. At the moment Rangda appears to win, a group of men, all entranced and wielding daggers, rush to Barong's aid. Rangda's witchcraft turns the men's blades against themselves in the fearful climax of the drama. These men in a cataleptic state engage in self-torture, and only the Barong's power saves them. There is no decisive resolution to this dance-drama — only a temporary victory for the forces of good and a short-lived abeyance of wickedness. Everyone goes home exhausted and relieved, knowing there will be more music and drama, more exuberance and excitement in the days to come.

Recognition of Bali's special place in world culture arrived slowly. In the 16th century Europe's great powers came to the East Indies in search of spices and colonial footholds. Portugal and Spain were first, followed soon after by Britain and Holland. There were certainly sightings of Bali by these foreigners, and even a landing in 1580 by the irrepressible Sir Francis Drake, but no written records of Bali were made until the final years of the 16th century. In 1597 a Dutch party came ashore and wrote the first detailed, though superficial, description of the island. For the next one-and-a-half centuries knowledge of Bali remained scant, with only occasional visits and commentaries by outsiders. In the mid-19th century things changed with the arrival of a profound Sanskrit scholar. That marked the beginning of serious study of Balinese culture, and there followed a string of excellent, dedicated Dutch academics who have continued their work up to the present day.

But the great age of Bali's blossoming, its 'opening' to the world, was in the 1930s. It was then that a small, influential group of Western artists, anthropologists, ethnomusicologists and novelists produced an outstanding body of work, sensitive and full of insight into Balinese life. Unfortunately among general readers the idea of Bali as Paradise developed, and this misreading was exacerbated by tour operators and cruise ships that brought tourists by the hundreds to gawp at bare-breasted maidens and take snapshots of 'temple dancers'. In addition, at about the same time, a series of sensationalist films on Bali became popular in Europe and North America. *Goona-goona* was the title of one of these films. It means 'magic' in Balinese, but became a slang term in New York for sex appeal.

As early as 1937 the writer Miguel Covarrubias, a keen observer and advocate of Balinese culture, predicted gloomily that the way of life 'is doomed to disappear under the merciless onslaught of modern commercialism and standardization'. Fifty years on, the question remains: 'Is Balinese culture already ruined or will it be able to withstand the onslaught of tourism?'. In some respects the question is moot, as such issues, vitally important to the Balinese, can only be answered by the local people themselves. For all the exotic characteristics of Balinese culture, it has one enduring and fundamental goal: balance and harmony within the natural and supernatural worlds. If the people of Bali can hold fast to this goal, no external force can defeat their spirit or way of life.

The real Bali does still exist, though the quality of this reality varies from place to place. The finest and truest the island has to offer will not appear effortlessly to the casual observer, though patience, care and understanding can help reveal Bali's magic. The pictures in this book are an affirmation, and their force and colour a small souvenir of a beautiful island.

An entrance tower guards the way to the royal palace of Puri Agung at Karengasem, east Bali. This was the site of the island's most important state in the late 18th and early 19th centuries. The tower and palace buildings are excellent examples of indigenous and imported architectural styles.

Following page
At Batuan, the famous cultural centre of central Bali, a procession winds its way through the paddy fields. These dancers form a gambuh *troupe; they perform one of the oldest dance-dramas on the island. It depicts chivalrous heroes and historical episodes from Bali's mythical past.*

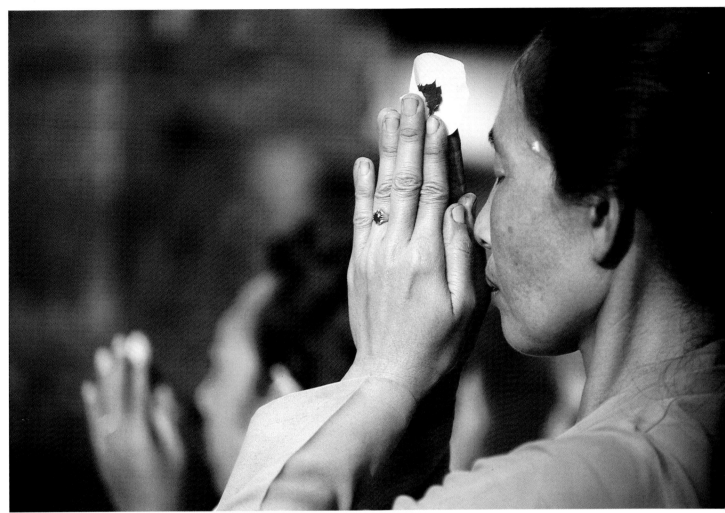

Preceding page
Warriors and brutish attendants march across a painted panel at the Hall of Justice, Klungkung. Vivid ceiling paintings show scenes from Heaven and Hell, symbolic of the rewards and punishments awaiting defendants. This was the highest court in the land during the 18th century.

In a moment of single-minded prayer, a woman presents a flower offering. As a gift to the gods, offerings must be pleasing but they can be as simple as a petal or a few grains of rice on a banana leaf. Each day of the week has its special spiritual attributes, and these determine what type, colour and form each offering should take.

Water from the jungly mountains streams through a temple complex of pagodas and pavilions. Channeled water and pools have always been a part of sacred sites, for purposes of washing and ritual cleansing.

Women wash clothes in the morning light of Lake Bratan, one of three lakes within a huge volcanic basin. Bali boasts four great volcanoes that stretch in a jumble from west to east, culminating in Gunung Agung, (right), the island's tallest and holiest.

Besakih Temple lies under the shadow of Gunung Agung at an altitude of 950 metres (3,000 feet). It represents the most sacred point of the compass for Balinese and has been a royal ancestral sanctuary since earliest times. Even the names of the gods enshrined here exist only in Old Balinese, predating influences from India or Java.

27

A girl of Ubud rests near a newly transplanted field of rice.

Harvesting rice is hard work, but the labour is done with happiness and a sense of anticipation of the coming festivals to celebrate the end of the rice cycle. In Bali three words for rice are used: padi, *origin of the English term* paddy, *indicates rice still in the field;* beras *means threshed rice; and* nasi *is the final form of the cooked, edible grain.*

Emerald fields of rice run through hills and valleys to the abrupt slopes of Gunung Batukau, a volcano that rises to 2,276 metres (7,467 feet). All parts of Bali that use irrigation are divided into units, and each of these local territories has its own temple and village organization to look after it.

Right
An 11-tiered meru *tower rises above the forest. These pagoda-like structures, a common feature of temple architecture, must have an odd number of storeys to fulfill their magical function of protection. Merus are symbolically associated with Gunung Agung, Mountain of the Gods. The little roofs are made of sugar-palm fibre and are sometimes covered with corrugated iron.*

A woman uses the evening breeze to help winnow rice.

A temple courtyard is used as a threshing ground. Once individual grains of rice have been separated from the ear they are swept up and bagged; they are then ready for sale or distribution before the final process of husking and polishing.

Left
The witch-widow Rangda, Goddess of Death and Queen of Evil Spirits, is seen in many forms on Bali: in paintings, in the dance-drama and, as here, in temple statuary. She represents the forces of darkness and harms the world with her black magic. Long fangs, bulging eyes and fiery tongue hanging between ugly, hairy breasts make her fearful, and youngsters especially are terrified by her reputation as a bloodthirsty child-eater.

Right
Three boys are safe in the doorway of a temple. The monumental gate is raised high on stone platforms and leads into the courtyard of the temple proper. The deity above the door appears malevolent, but he is in fact a protector and will hurt only those who enter with evil intentions.

Following page
Intricate, gaudy offerings called tjilis are made of moulded, fried rice flour, dyed with brilliant colours and embellished with flowers.

Above
A group of women shares a joke while working together to make temple offerings. This is a time to gossip and relax while doing something useful for the community. Stripped palm fronds will be folded and pinned to create lamaks, pretty, perishable decorations (right) that usually only last one day before becoming wilted and spent.

Left and far right
Sometimes detailed, other times stylized and made of simple palm leaves (page 38), tjilis represent beautiful girls with slender bodies and large headdresses. Their origins can be traced back to primitive rites that honoured the deities of rice and fertility.

Solemnity marks the beginning of the
Tooth Filing Ceremony, usually conducted
when the young approach puberty. A priest
leads the ceremony, and at its climax the
initiates lie down and have their teeth filed
into neat, clean rows. This is a symbolic
purification. By removing all points and
rough edges of the teeth, the filing ritually
overcomes the base characteristics of greed,
sloth, hatred and ignorance, preparing the
youngster to take part in the full life of the
community.

A temple festival takes place at Bangli. This
temple, Pura Kehan, has a history of 800
years and is a fine example of the southern
style of architecture. It is built of reddish-
pink brick and has intricate carvings in
grey and pink sandstone.

A huge procession forms part of the odalan, *a celebration to mark the village temple's anniversary. Days of preparation go into a successful* odalan *and the culmination is this march to the sea where statues of the temple gods will be given a ritual bath. Women (above) with waists wrapped in beautiful saffron scarves carry offerings of cloth, flowers, fruit and holy water. Gongs and orchestral music accompany the general noise and gaiety of the crowd.*

A concerned onlooker watches as a group of young men lose control in a state of trance. Friends and caretakers of the trance ceremony keep them from hurting themselves or people in the crowd. Trance is not at all unusual in Bali; it is encouraged as a special state in which people can enter into direct communication with the spirit world and bring back knowledge or special wishes of the deities. Even in moments of ecstasy or self-inflicted violence, trance is rarely allowed to get out of control.

On foot and in overloaded boats, crowds of people head off for a festival at the temple of Pura Sakenan, a holy site for the people of southern Bali. It sits on the shore of Serangan, better known as Turtle Island for its huge sea turtles. These are especially prized as food for village feasts.

Following page
Tall banners stand before the temple of Tanah Lot. This small, beautifully located temple was built in the 16th century by Sang Hiyang Nirartha, the last important priest to come to Bali from Java. He arrived to strengthen the island's Hindu faith, and Tanah Lot is a memorial to his efforts.

47

A B
to c
fron
for
the
the

Preceding page
Balinese masks are carved realistically, full of human feeling and expressiveness. A good set of masks is a treasure for the community lucky enough to own it. The most famous mask-dance is the topeng, *which means literally 'something pressed against the face'.*

Shadow puppets, seen in profile and projected onto a screen by the light of an oil lamp, are made of thinly cut buffalo skin, painted and gilded to wonderful effect. Known as wayang kulit, *stage performances of these shadow puppets are the main medium for classical poetry and epic history, all important in the spiritual education of the common people.*

A young baris *dancer strikes a martial pose. The* baris *is a ritual war dance, stately and full of pomp. It is an expression of manly attributes and was the precursor of all male dances on Bali. Performers must be fit as all parts of the body, from the forehead to the toes, are used in action. Music always accompanies the* baris, *and the relation of dance to music is close, with many changes of mood and expression.*

Two girls dance with all the skill and concentration they possess. Dance training begins at an early age and requires years of rigorous training. At first, a teacher guides the girls through the movements, leading them by the wrists again and again until the entire choreography is an indelible part of them.

A young Legong dancer.

The dance-pantomime known as legong is the best loved of classical dances in Bali. Only girls perform the legong, often beginning their training at age five. By 14 they are too old and retire forever from this style of dancing. The girls are called 'divine nymphs' and act the roles of highly refined courtiers.

Janger dancers with remarkable florid head-dresses move across a temple courtyard. The dance began around 1925 and was strongly influenced by Malay opera. It was also the first social dance in Bali where boys and girls could join together and have fun. The janger had a brief and glorious period, epitomizing the Balinese love of new things, but today it is performed mostly for tourists.

Following page
The kecak *is a dance with large groups of men singing, chanting and moving together with the music. The best known* kecak *accompanies stories from the Ramayana, the great Hindu epic, and trance dancing is frequently an element of these performances. It is also known as the Monkey Dance, named for an episode where the male chorus plays a jabbering band of monkeys in thrall of its leader, Hanuman, the Monkey King.*

61

The gamelan, *a percussion orchestra made up primarily of metallophones, numerous suspended gongs and many types of cymbals, is an indispensable part of Balinese creative life. Most villages have one or two* gamelan *orchestras, and the strange music with its subtle beauty can be heard throughout the island nearly every evening. The bamboo flute (right) is used as a lead for the melody.*

Bali's most powerful drama revolves around the confrontation and clash of two mythical creatures, Barong and Rangda, personifications of the forces of good and evil. The Barong (left) is a lion-beast that represents sunshine, medicine, life and light. Despite his fierce look he is the antidote for evil and he likes to dance for the sheer joy of entertainment.

But Barong's playfulness is interrupted by the appearance of Rangda, hideous witch and Queen of Death. In the climactic struggle that ensues, trance dancers rush to Barongs aid, only to have their daggers turned against themselves by Rangda's evil magic (right). Barong's own power prevents the daggers from piercing flesh no matter how the entranced men try to kill themselves. In the end the dancers are slowly brought out of trance with the aid of Barong's beard, his centre of power. There is no ultimate winner in the cosmic struggle; goodness gains only a temporary victory and evil invariably engages in the battle again.

Every third day is a major market day on Bali. Traditionally, women control the goods and do nearly all the buying and selling. They stream into towns in the morning and by noon the activity is at its height, the marketplace filled with exotic smells of pepper, cinnamon, mace, coconut oil, dried fish and fried sweetbreads. Two women (above) relax at the end of a market day.

Bali, covering just over 2,000
square miles in area, has a
population of nearly three
million inhabitants. The
Balinese people are known for
their gentleness, humour and
creativity.

A mask-maker from Mas shows off one of his works. In former times the famous artists of this region worked solely for the temples and royal courts. Nowadays secular art is widespread and masks can be made for pleasure and sold commercially

An artist emerges from behind two panels of his forest painting. Painting in Bali went through a period of rejuvenation in the 1930s when it was strongly influenced and encouraged by European artists. They introduced new materials, themes and treatment of light and helped liberate painting from static, traditional forms.

For more than 50 years tourists have been
coming to Bali to play, to relax, to learn
and to share in the special magic of the
island. A family (above) makes its way past
the limestone caves of Ulu Watu.

A young traveller (left) chats about surfing
with a local boy.

Balinese and tourists alike love the kites and kite festivals along the beaches.

Clouds pile up along the coast
as a solitary walker shares in
the peaceful end of a day.

A boy holds his kite proudly
before letting it soar into the
evening sky.

Following page
A purple sunset descends on
Candi Dasa, an ancient
settlement in Tenganan District,
northeast Bali.